Tom de Toys
alias Tomithy Holeapple

THE VERY MOMENT

27 english poems

1998 – 2020

Ed. G&GN institute
© POEMiE™

TOM DE TOYS (real name: Thomas Holzapfel = Crabapple): the author of the german book *"MORE NOW – CHANGE OF CONSCIOUSNESS FROM SYMBOLICITY TO PRESENTICITY"* was born in Jülich (Germany) in 1968 and lived from 1997 til 2012 in Berlin. He published "Direct Poetry" (poetology of transreligious holEism) under more than 40 pseudonyms for almost three decades. Since 1989 he works actively both as a painter and as a performance artist for the philosophy of holEism. In 1990 he founded the so-called G&GN-Institut ("Institute For Complete Nothing@All"). In 1994 he discovered the theory of E.S. ("Extended Sobriety") whereby authentic (i.e. fulfilled) love poetry can be politicised against the conventional misuse of the expression "love" (as in 95% of all fake love poems "longing" is meant indeed). In 2000 he received the very first NAHBELL prize, a kind of alternative Nobel Prize for german contemporary poetry. In 2001 he invented QUANTUM POETRY which was world-premièred at the university of São Paulo (thanks to Goethe-Institut). Since 2012 De Toys lives in the district Eller Süd of Düsseldorf. His german poetry works as well as his photo art and landscape drawings appear already in many themed compilations (all available books @ www.neurogermanistik.de). Since 1998 De Toys writes short poems and english poems once in a while under the pseudonym of **Tomithy Holeapple** who translated also some pieces of his german oeuvre. In 2019, after a thirty year break, he started playing free jazz piano again: NONDUALJAZZ.de

The **G&GN-Institut** ("Institute For Complete Nothing@All") was founded in 1990 as an independent publisher and organizer within the german scene of underground literature. In 2017 the 3rd festival for so-called "off poetry" was managed by G&GN powered by the Ministry for Family Affairs. His catalogue of questions about the participating authors is accepted by the Ministry for School and Education in North Rhine-Westphalia to be used as teaching aids in lessons about live poetry: LYRIKFESTIVAL.de

© SECOND EDITION 2020
ISBN 9783743159617
Manufacturing and publisher: BoD
Books on Demand, Norderstedt, Germany

"...all aspects of the world become meaningful rather than meaningless. This is not to say that they acquire meaning in the sense of signs, by virtue of pointing to something else, but that all things appear to be their own point. Their simple existence, or better, their present formation, seems to be perfect, to be an end or fulfillment without any need for justification. Flowers do not bloom in order to produce seeds, nor are seeds germinated in order to bring forth flowers. Each stage of the process – seed, sprout, bud, flower, and fruit – may be regarded as the goal."

**Alan Watts, 1958:
THIS IS IT**

CONTENT
© www.poem2go.de

01) **23.7.1998**: WIN
02) **17.1.1999**: SIN
03) **12.12.2004**: MAKiNG LOV!NG
04) **15.12.2008**: GOLDsNOW
05) **19.12.2008**: SECRET (K)NOWLEDGE (MiSSiNG LiNK)
06) **23.1.2009**: OVERWOR(L)DED (BE-ing NOWhere)
[12th PRAYER OF TRANSRELIGIOUS HOLeISM]
07) **24.+28.1.2009**:
SUPERFLUOUS HOLeIDAY BEAT (MADe PeACE BY THE PIECE)
[13th PRAYER OF TRANSRELIGIOUS HOLeISM]
08) **2./3.2.2009**: SUperroutiNe (HAPPY-GO-LUCKY-GOA[L])
09) **21.4.2009**: OVERSHiNiNG
10) **27.-29.4.2009**:
GÖTTLICHES FALLOBST (SHAKE OFF THE DIVINE PEAR)
11) **8.5.2009**:
present poWEr poINt of vision (autOMatic atOMizer)
12) **24.5.2009**: WE ARE THE ZENSE OF LIFE
13) **4.6.2009**: GOLDEN-LIGHT DRUNKEN DISTRICT
(iN My VeRy MeMoRy oF NoWaDayS)
14) **4.8.2009**: COSMIC OCEAN (Several Suns Say Shine)
15) **11.+13.8.2009**: B(L)OW UP A DOzen TIMES
16) **5.12.2009**: EXTENDED EXPRESSION OF A SYSTEMLESS SOUL
[16th PRAYER OF TRANSRELIGIOUS HOLeISM]
17) **15.12.2009**:
BEYOND THE MATRIX OF METAPHYSICAL MADNESS
18) **3.3.2012**: RESISTANT RESISTANCE
(A CUP OF POETRY TO RUN & BITE)
19) **22.9.2012**:
(C)OMPETITION (A VERY LONG SHORT-POEM)
20) **16.5.2013**: NASTY TONGUES OF NOBLE ANGELS
21) **17.+29.7.2014**:
SOUL COLLECTION/GATHERING
22) **15.7.2015**: TWEENKLE
23) **3.7.2016**: IDONTITY
24) **5.9.2016**: DIGITAL GAME OF IDENTITY
25) **16.2.2017**: W(O/A)NDERING
26) **6.4.2020**: MY BOREOUT YOGA
27) **10.5.2020**: THE SURPASSED ONES (ÜBERTROFFENE, 110.E.S.)

Tom MöDE

WIN

you come when
i calculate with
all but you
and stay
as if i
was never
without you

SIN

i believe in us
because we live
nothing is surer
than each breath
that connects me
with you like a
distant kiss

MAKiNG LOV!NG

you wonna love poem?
are you sure?
a real love poem?
i mean: A poem
where love does happen?
i tell you something
(NO STORY – SORRY !)
Making all that Loving
you need for writing
a super real love poem
is harder than heaven
never a joke but
much much soul
fucking
fun
(know what i mean?)

GOLDsNOW

how peaceful how white
this winter awakes
in soft morning light
no real horizon found
where silence turns
to unexpected sound
no heaven no ground
just golden snow
to show you
the middle of now

SECRET (K)NOWLEDGE
(MiSSiNG LiNK)

i miss u yes i do i do
i miss u yes i do
i miss u darling
and i like it yes
i like to miss u
cause i know it's u
it's u my star
it's u my sun
my life is lucky
since i know u a
reality reality
no need to flee
no need to flee
i want to be
with u with u
no reason why
no reason WHO
I AM without u
who i am
it's up to u
if i miss u
i miss u YES I DO
i do

OVERWOR(L)DED
(BE-ing NOWhere)
[12th PRAYER OF TRANSRELIGIOUS HOLeISM]

no sun no moon no galaxy
no thoughts of nothing and
no nothing no illusions and
no truth no question but
no need for answers
is the answer just
awake aware arrived
where this is
called the only THIS
AND THAT is sure
like nothing more than THIS
AND THAT turns mad
if you cant love it
like the laughter
of your lover
of your laughter
til the end of time
within this mOMent
that is touching
as you know it
now from inside
where the emptiness
turns outside
showing this is
no side never

SUPERFLUOUS HOLeIDAY BEAT
(MADe PeACE BY THE PIECE)
[13th PRAYER OF TRANSRELIGIOUS HOLeISM]

no accident
by accident no birth
no death no guarantee
no time to grow into the show
no ground no reason no season to flee
no flower no power no soul to be shy and no
hole to ask why this old flowerpot is empty and
no flower-beds nowhere to sleep away over roses
no flow to fly no flop no disc no floppy jockey yes no joke
awoke no superwhoops to die OFF...LINE and out no shout
no shit by the way no way out of the way to cry for
hollow holiness for heroes to excuse the crime
no following to follow the following no
longing no belonging no beloved
no bench to sit no goal to hit
no bell to ring no song to
sing no angel wing no
Peace no War
no worship
and no
law
no
starship
and no rush
no hour but no hush
no shower gets on down

your nerves no worldwide wisdom
curves the never-ending universe no world
no power no world power no world record and no
game to play no run away no fun to stay no lessions
to teach about no level to reach no links to link at
the cosmic beach no drowning of no waters to
waste no wasteland to watch no watch to
wait no Love no Hate no artless piece no
arty peace to piece together peace to-
gether no no no no moment for no
compliment is left to say you are
DOWNLOADED down-to-earth
down right because we
share no ray of hope
we are at the end of
our rope we are
enlightened we
are engaged
we are
that
stupid
STREAM of
middle-aged
consciousness
but no new age
no secrets in a flash
of lightning no security
beyond the light no letters
to write no head to head no
hand to hand no hole to hold the
line to drop a line between the lines

SuperroutiNe
(HAPPY-GO-LUCKY-GOA[L])

and even if
we cannot meet
BEfore our skins get dry
i swear it is a fun
to wait for you
BEcause the tears of happiness
for just one holy day
in paradise on earth
will heal us
like the cosmic waters
that were flowing through
our letters out of time
it is for sure that we
BElong to those who lived
at least in this same century
to touch the other soul
not only with remembrances but
yes by holding hands and
kissing speechless lips
until the planet takes our bodies back
to keep the weight
to stay on our routine trip
BEtween the stars
we never reach and
nevertheless enjoy
this single second
BEing present part of a

cOMpleted system of cOMmunication
inBEtween eternal levels
that are made of energy
to love its own existence
through its empty cells of
consciousness

OVERSHiNiNG

brains breathing
coreless through the hollow
body glows
the cosmic
carrousel of lights

GÖTTLICHES FALLOBST
(SHAKE OFF THE DIVINE PEAR)

und die engel bluten weiter
jeder stern entpuppt sich gern als hohle hürde und
die liebe folgt nur diesem quantenoptischen prozess
aus bunten nullen und schwarzweißen einsen
wir sind nicht nur fremde sogar in der heimat
hat der tod seinen sonderpreis und fordert würde

and the angels don't stop bleeding
each star likes to turn out to be a hollow hurdle and
love follows just these quantum-optical processes
made of blackwhite ones and colored zeros
we are not just strangers even at home
death demands a special price and dignity

present poWEr poINt of vision
(autOMatic atOMizer)

people pretend
to Be positive
to enable you sOMehow
embracing their so-called
enlightened emptiness
that develops
into a special hell
instead of the big hole
where we meet
our mutual spirit
by passing through
nuclear-free love
as soul sisters
oh yes it is seldOM
i kNOW it but
well i believe in this
This without any belief

WE ARE THE ZENSE OF LIFE

birds are chirping
water flows
wind is rushing
through the leaves
i am sitting here
and reading this

GOLDEN-LIGHT DRUNKEN DISTRICT
(iN My VeRy MeMoRy oF NoWaDayS)

ten years ago it was just
another district in the same city
a red wine a beer and a cigarette
twenty years ago it was another city but the
same district a red wine a beer and a cigarette
so i finished my work yes as soon as possible
although really nobody needs it til now just now
who needs art anyway if it shall change the world
you can sell it far out if you belong to a system
but do not believe it means any big change
when you become part of that structure
you never agreed in your soul because
your soul needs no structure it is
a structure-free zone it is
speechless and empty
made of an infinite
hollow throne

COSMIC OCEAN
(Several Suns Say Shine)

a very normal day on this planet earth and the sun shines on the waters like a million galaxies i say yes THE SUN SHINES LIKE GALAXIES there are billions of stars shining thru our one and only own sun i love you sun i need you sun you are my biggest love i say yes THE SUN IS MY BIGGEST LOVE as long as i am alive and what happens afterwards is not my problem it is just the solution the sun is my very now being a real being being a life alive a life alive a simple single sun i say each human is a sun is a sun each human is more than just a human is a sun is a billion of suns is a galaxy is a whole and holy infinite universe each human is even more than universe is a part of the emptiness flowing thru it all like the waters flowing thru the brains like the energy flowing invisible thru it all thru it all thru the emptiness i say look thru the emptiness LOOK THRU THE EMPTINESS can you see any other side of the emptiness of the universe of the sun can you see the sun from the other side of the universe come on tell me if you know something tell it to the world we need your wisdom our presidents need it so much yes they need you they need us they need such enlightened beings that know that we ARE alive that we SEE the sun that we KNOW how big universe REALLY is and how crazy THE OTHER SIDE OF INFINITY feels yes we feel it and yes we want it and yes we need no more drugs to excuse our point of no points of view of points of stars of points of light of points of points of nowadays is now a days is NOW a DAYS is nowadays nowadays nooooow aaaaaa daaaayyyyyssssssssss

B(L)OW UP A DOzen TIMES

i turn around
to you who turns
around to me
so that we see each
other through the empty
space to drop
out of the show in
between the dream
was just a doze
before we follow
the trace of a cosmic
race if we gather
our souls like boulders
no need to wait for
the stars cannot hesitate
to shine right now
wherever we go
we bow to the break
to blow up the fake
and grow into
the slow motion
matter of facts

EXTENDED EXPRESSION OF A SYSTEMLESS SOUL
[16th PRAYER OF TRANSRELIGIOUS HOLeISM]

i am
circling
around
my empty
center of
gravity

BEYOND THE MATRIX OF METAPHYSICAL MADNESS

if you want to find Friends:
BE FRIENDLY!
if you want to feel Love:
BE LOVELY!
if you want to meet God:
BE GORGEOUS!
but if you want to know
more than this simple
matrix of madness
just to discover
eternal emptiness:
STOP WANTING!
and return to the infinite
nature of existence...

RESISTANT RESISTANCE
(A CUP OF POETRY TO RUN & BITE)

i like to share my thoughts
because they are no lords
in those i believe
shall be my teeth
to read some truth
standing on the roof
where stars are hit
i feel spirit
flowing in poetry
no rules to flee
no fools for tea
we run away
and bite the ray
of light in brains
to overcome
the normal pains

(C)OMPETITION
(A VERY LONG SHORT-POEM)

you're neither devil nor god
you are neither angel nor animal
you're somehow wise but unknown
as well called a human
so-called being but indeed
these are just names
like frames for your brains
to follow in chains
as long as it rains
til your eyes rise with the sun
and your heart tries to have fun
until master death stops
the run – well-done!

NASTY TONGUES OF NOBLE ANGELS

W
HAT
IS A
GO(O)D
POEM? WHY
B(R)OTHER?

SOUL COLLECTION/GATHERING

nobody
exists
we can
start

TWEENKLE

THIS
POEM
PROVES
THE
EXISTENCE
OF
POETRY

IDONTITY

universe walks
on two feet
thru itself

DIGITAL GAME OF IDENTITY

all pictures
deleted again
here and now
the very moment
can start

W(O/A)NDERING

To write a poem is what i would like
But all i find are brutal words
By money people that don't hike
Thru feelings in a world that hurts

MY BOREOUT YOGA

i am neither a bird singing
a beautiful song to entertain you
nor a poet that stopped writing poetry
after Auschwitz i am just a normal human
being in quarantine because of that
panicked corona pandemic and i do
not speak english or german or chinese
but the language of my soul that is
silence at a very deep point of no return
in my shocking hollow bones since i
feel that i am made of total emptiness
without any fitting description to make
you understand how it feels when your
dissolved identity talks to you as a ghost
in a black business suit while you yourself
became identical with the air and the sun
and the most distant galaxies everything
seems to be somehow connected and
nothing seems to be somewhere beyond
universe i feel life here exactly here
as an absolute inside job right now
in my little room where i stay during
the infinite moment of days and weeks
and months of waiting to meet you again
my beloved friend just to prove that
i was able to taste your kiss indeed
all the time thinking of you

THE SURPASSED ONES
*(110th example for Extended Sobriety
dedicated to Barbara, published @ pendemic.ie)*

your voice producing world
literature indeed our ssweat
so ssweet and spicy capable
to resist the spelling reform as
well as the pandemic rules of
distance some flowers start to
grow grammatically correct on
our bodies in a poetry-free space
this scent is dictated by life we
are surpassing our own fan-
tasies about the other gender

ÜBERTROFFENE
(110.E.S. für Barbara)

deine stimme produziert weltliteratur
unser schweißß widersetzt sich
süßßlich-scharf
der rechtschreibreform und den
pandemischen abstandsregeln
auf unseren körpern wachsen
grammatisch korrekte blumen
das leben diktiert diesen duft im
poesiefreien zwischenraum wir
übertreffen unsere eigenen fan-
tasien über das andere geschlecht

"...the monster poet – mostly he works himself up into some kind of ecstasy: the pioneer of consciousness wants to overcome by means of his art any sort of religion..."
FAZ 1997

"...the one with his 'Unprovoked Appresence' whose essential message is eternal presence..."
taz 1999

Brand-new in 2020: secondary literature!

All my books @ www.neurogermanistik.de